THE
BLUFFER'S GUIDE®
TO
SECRETARIES

SUE DYSON

G000135949

Oval Books

Published by Oval Books
335 Kennington Road
London SE11 4QE
United Kingdom

Telephone: +44 (0)20 7582 7123
Fax: +44 (0)20 7582 1022
E-mail: info@ovalbooks.com

First published by Ravette Publishing, 1989
New edition published by Oval Books, 2000

Series Editor – Anne Tauté

Cover designer – Jim Wire, Quantum
Printer – Cox & Wyman Ltd
Producer – Oval Projects Ltd

The Bluffer's Guides® series is based
on an original idea by Peter Wolfe.

ISBN: 1-902825-59-4

CONTENTS

INTRODUCTION

Managers seem to think that secretaries are like gun dogs: excellent working animals, tireless and loyal if properly trained – and a real liability if given their head. Secretaries know that their bosses have got the wrong end of the stick: it is managers who need a disciplined training programme, and managers who have that unique capacity for disruption if allowed to slip their collars for ten minutes.

Office life can be a bit of a cat-and-mouse game: an eternal chase for power and points. If the manager and secretary are Tom and Jerry, this book is strictly for the mouse. Bluffers should remember: Jerry always gets the upper hand in the end.

Companies like to talk about training their secretaries to work for management. In reality you are the one who does all the training, because a well-trained manager is your passport to a happy working life. You will be the envy of all the other secretaries whose bosses are completely untamed; and since your boss thinks he or she can't manage without you, you shouldn't have any trouble getting a rise.

Most managers only survive by bluff. The professional secretary is much more intelligent and can turn bluff into an art form. The name of the game is to control your boss's life, thoughts and behaviour, since he or she is your ticket to a brilliant career – or the start of a new job search.

And you have to learn to play the organisation game, too. If you're infinitely ambitious but lack deviousness, read on – but don't make the mistake of letting your boss get his hands on this book.

If, on the other hand, you are already PA to the Chairman of Megamoney Plc, congratulations. This time next year you might be Chairman.

SECRETARIES AT WORK

If you want to climb to the top of the tree, first of all you have to promote yourself. If you don't blow your own trumpet, nobody else is going to do it for you.

Secretaries have long laboured under the image of an expensive status symbol, and bosses are always on the lookout for new and better ways of adding to the size of their own egos, via their secretaries. Some of the more well-worn techniques are:

a) purchasing the very latest high-tech equipment, whether or not it is appropriate or compatible (good bluffers should always watch for signs of imminent spending sprees, and demand to be consulted)

b) giving out a plethora of 'perks' – free lunches, time off, travel discounts, clothes allowance and so on. (They will boast about these to their friends, and you will have to say how grateful you are, even if you aren't.)

c) sending you on a succession of training courses. Some of these courses may help the secretary's career or add to personal skills, but most of them are not much better than a day out at the races, which you might well have enjoyed more.

The main thing to remember about secretarial work is that no two jobs are the same. This gives you ample opportunity to act the innocent until you have been in a new job long enough to be genuinely efficient.

The description 'secretary' can be applied to anyone from a junior typist to a management assistant, because nobody has yet come up with a definition which is generally acceptable. Many managers like to call their clerical assistants 'secretaries' because then they can inflate their own egos at business lunches by remarking carelessly, "I'll get my secretary to do that", or "Just give my secretary a call".

This gives you the ideal opportunity to upgrade your job title from WP operator to Assistant Office Systems Manager, from junior shorthand typist to Executive PA – or anything else you fancy. Just pray that no-one realises your own experience of the job amounts to stage one typing and six months' invoice-checking in a marmalade factory.

Getting Qualified

Some of the top secretaries around have hardly a qualification to their name. Unfortunately for the dedicated bluffer, it is just not enough any more. The system of vocational qualifications (NVQs) means that, in line with the rest of Europe, there is more studying for everyone. Even if you never manage to get that coveted high-level NVQ, you should be seen to make an attempt.

A good ploy is to say that you are "between levels" – and on the way up. Your boss will think you are striving away industriously to accumulate your 'credits', whereas in fact the only credits you take notice of are the ones written large on the cinema screen.

Once qualified you can expect to join one of the many professional associations for secretaries: maybe the Institute of Qualified Private Secretaries, or the European Association of Professional Secretaries. Whether it is worth it depends on what you are looking for. On the plus side:

- you will get an impressive-looking array of letters after your name
- you will get invited to social functions and professional conferences
- you will meet other amazingly well-qualified secretaries and may get an even better job through your contacts
- you may get specialised training or tuition at reduced rates
- you will get the chance to advertise how well qualified you are by buying a variety of distinctive merchandise: imitation marble pen-holders, headscarves and desk sets, covered in mauve logos.

On the down side:

- you will have to pay an annual subscription, plus the exorbitant cost of any functions you attend. Count this as an investment.
- you may make your boss wary if you appear 'over-qualified'. Some may be put off employing you if they think you are so good that you will demand an astronomic salary or become better-qualified than they are.
- you will land yourself with things covered with mauve logos.

Of course, there is always the easy way out. Saying that you have taken such and such a course never fails to impress, and few will question whether you have obtained the requisite certificates. One enthusiast carried a piece of paper around for years which was never queried by prospective employers. Signed by the principal, it stated that she had studied 12 subjects at commercial college. What it did not state was that she had failed them all.

Trendy Training

Whether or not you have actually been on any training course is relatively unimportant. What really matters is your ability to convince people that you have. Casual but confident comment about "skills inventories" or "energy curves" should be more than enough to wrong-foot any rival, and quite a few managers too.

It is good for your image. It can also give your manager much-needed status. To a boss, sending a secretary on a succession of privately-run, rather exclusive and extremely expensive courses is an indicator to other bosses that:

- my secretary is a high-flier (much better than yours)
- I am generous and am prepared to manage without my excellent secretary for half a day because I care about my subordinates and their career aspirations (I can always borrow your secretary)
- I am important, and can pull strings
- I am a forward-thinking sort of manager, keen to move with the times (at least until my secretary asks for secondment to study for an MBA).

You have two options: to take in the occasional course, or to bluff. It all depends on how much you want to get out of the office. Either way, you need to know some relevant facts, and a little background on the trainers who run the courses is a must.

These are people with titles like 'Industrial Training Expert', 'Management Training Consultant' or 'Leadership Skills Adviser': people who charge high fees and have an inflated opinion of their own importance. They claim to be at a loss to understand how the untrained masses ever manage to organise getting out of bed, though they will nevertheless try to persuade you that the most humble job (manning the tea trolley) represents an important contribution to management.

However, you should know that the typical management trainer is a failed manager who picks up a golden handshake and starts a management training consultancy. It is the easiest thing in the world: all that is needed is a big bundle of glossy leaflets and a hired conference room. The world is simply packed full of ambitious young secretaries, desperate to get on, who firmly believe their best chance of getting to the top is to go on an upmarket course. They may be right. Anything with 'management' in the title (e.g. 'Time Management') sounds impressive and you don't have to take any irksome exams.

A true bluffer will take the process one step further: if you are going to eliminate the exams, why not eliminate the course as well? Simply lead everyone to believe you have been on a course, and the effect should be the same. Take your pick from the following:

Self-assertion – Bossiness, tempered with low cunning. Trendy trainers will deny this, but self-assertion courses are basically about getting your own way – an essential skill for the dedicated bluffer, best acquired through an in-depth understanding of your boss's weaknesses.

Management for Secretaries – Not much use unless you want to remain a secretary. Better to gain prestige by letting everyone think you have been on a straightforward 'management' course (leave out the secretaries bit). This way, you will be seen as management potential, rather than as a secretary desperately trying to convince everyone that she is a manager in her own right. Beware the insecure boss whose ploy is to keep you quiet rather than provide you with a dynamic addition to your CV.

Specialist Courses (e.g. 'Personnel for Secretaries') – These are the 'bread and butter' courses – they try to teach you how to do your job properly. Hard work, so not recommended for serious bluffers. Not much prestige, either.

Self-defence – Not one of the easiest to bluff about. A female secretary who lets it be known that she has been on a self-defence course is liable to inspire some very mixed feelings in her male colleagues. They may flinch from you as you walk down the corridor. Watch out for the amateur Rambo who leaps out from behind every filing cabinet, jeering and inviting you to wrestle him to the ground.

Languages for Business – Courses that sound like a good idea but involve being cooped up in a language laboratory for days on end trying to master the German for prefabricated pre-stressed concrete. In any case, bi-lingual secretaries don't earn a fortune, so is it really worth all the agony. If you can say "How are you?" and "Would you like a coffee?" in eight languages, that should see you through nicely and impress your boss no end.

Stress Management – This is a good one to bluff about because it's so vague. Just mutter a few words about "the time/change continuum", and no-one will suspect a thing. What's more, your colleagues will be thoroughly impressed to know that your job is so high-powered that you need to go on a course to learn how to cope with the stress.

Time Management – The big one. This is the star of trendy training programmes. Everyone wants a piece of the action, and if you haven't been on a time management course yet, you had better start bluffing right away. What time management really means is 'getting your act together' – no more and no less. So if you can fathom the intricacies of the office diary, organise your workload so that everything isn't left until Friday afternoon, and delegate work to your boss, you are an effective time manager.

Hopeless time managers are people who habitually chair meetings lasting five hours and are never really clear about what they are trying to achieve. Most good time managers are secretaries: untrained bosses fondly imagine they don't need to sort themselves out because they have secretaries to do it for them.

If you are even a reasonably efficient secretary, you are a good time manager – so there is no need to waste valuable time by going on this course. Just remember these useful words and phrases, and use them at strategic moments in your conversation:

- "I need a few hours to rationalise my time log."
- "Effective life planning is all about setting one's strategic goals, don't you think?"
- "I feel there's some room for improvement in your deskmanship."
- "I'm a little concerned about the departmental planning-implementation ratio."

The Art of Looking Busy

Many ambitious secretaries suffer from an unfortunate affliction: they are too conscientious for their own good. They seem to believe that, since they are paid tolerably well and are on the look-out for promotion, they have to be busy all the time.

The bluffer knows that no-one – not even a secretary – can produce the same degree of concentration and effort all day long. A survey has indicated that office productivity fluctuates wildly according to the time of day and the day of the week. The peak of activity comes, apparently, somewhere between 11 a.m. and 1 p.m. on a Tuesday – and it's all downhill from there on.

Everyone finds a new job stressful and difficult, but if you are still having to put in a huge amount of effort after six months, you should be looking for a reason. Consider the following:

1. You may be in the wrong job. We can't all aspire to be Management Assistant to the Chairman of ICI, nor do we all have an aptitude for figure work, shorthand or the law. There are lots of other secretarial jobs around, and sometimes opportunities to move out of secretarial work altogether.

2. You have the wrong approach. It could be that you are inventing unnecessary tasks or refusing to delegate, for example, to your boss.

3. You feel guilty if you aren't doing something, so you willingly take on extra work. Not surprisingly, once they have got over the initial shock, others will be only too happy to offload all those boring jobs they have been putting off for months on to you.

4. Your boss is a lazy swine.

Never allow yourself to become the office workhorse: the people who have the greatest career success are rarely the people who work the hardest. If you do, the day will come when the volume of your own work reaches overload proportions, but you are cornered because you have agreed to do half of everybody else's jobs too. So while you are hurtling around with the sweat melting your mascara, your colleagues are lounging around with their feet on the desks, gossiping and eating sticky buns.

Note that when you ask them if they could possibly help you out, they will remember 101 urgent tasks which they cannot possibly put off. The laws of 'boom and slump' apply not only to the economy but also to a secretary's workload. Some days you will be teetering on the brink of nervous exhaustion. At other times you will have a nagging feeling of doubt: have you forgotten to do something vital and terribly obvious? Is your work full of mistakes because you rushed it? Relax. Having nothing to do is normal – so long as it only happens some of the time.

The important things to remember are:

1. Always look busy. Whether you really are busy or not doesn't matter: the essential thing is never to look as if you have nothing to do. Top secretaries prioritise their work, and manage their time so that there is always some on-going task to resort to when there isn't much else to do.

2. Keep a stock of non-urgent work in your desk – things which have to be done sometime but have no particular deadline, and which can be carried out piecemeal on 'quiet' days. That way, you can always avoid the cardinal sin of appearing to be totally idle.

3. If you resort to reading a book or playing with your GameBoy, at least make sure that something impressive is displayed on your screen (which you will of course angle towards the door or window so that passers-by can see how hard you are working). Slipping your bestseller inside the covers of the company's latest annual report will also help safeguard your image.

4. If you have to leave the office on an important expedition (to get a doughnut), carry a file or notebook with you.

5. Never tell your boss you have nothing to do. Your boss will feel obliged to add to your in-tray and one day you will find you have accumulated so much that you can't cope any more. In extreme circumstances, your boss may even question the need to employ a secretary at all.

Your Image

It used to be said that smart people wore suits, and were ultra conventional in their choice of clothes. This is no longer true: some of the big names in business look like a random assortment of jumble and no-one would question their talent.

Whatever you choose to wear, the simple rules for creating a successful image are:

1. Never look grubby. The day you ignore an egg stain on your shirt front is bound to be the day an unexpected meeting is held and you are in the spotlight.

2. If you got to bed at 3 a.m., make sure you don't look that way. Give yourself extra time to prepare. You may feel like death, but it pays not to look like it.

If you are determined to dress like Zandra Rhodes or Richard Branson, you just have to work twice as hard. Male secretaries can get away with less effort (nail varnish and eye make-up optional).

The Secretary's Survival Kit

Every top secretary has to have a 'bottom drawer'. Experienced bluffers will know that this is not some devious preparation for the day when a boss caves in and proposes marriage. It is an Aladdin's cave of survival gear – the secretarial equivalent of a life raft, iron rations and a packet of distress flares.

Professional secretaries are problem solvers. They have to be, because – for all their boasts – managers are generally useless in the face of everyday calamities. They know what to do when confronted with a takeover bid, but just wait for the expression of panic when they lose a button from a jacket, or forget an anniversary.

Female bosses probably have a greater aptitude for dealing with day-to-day problems than male bosses, but in practice it makes little difference because they usually think they are above such matters. The ones who used to be secretaries themselves can be particularly firm in their belief that it is the secretary's sole responsibility to avert impending disaster. There is none so keen as the poacher turned gamekeeper.

Your survival kit will probably need to contain most of the following:

- scissors
- needle and thread (navy, grey, black, white plus brighter shades if you have a female boss)
- safety pins
- spare set of boss's car keys
- boss's blood pressure tablets – and your own
- sticking plasters
- paracetamol tablets
- spare tights
- a soft toilet roll (has umpteen uses apart from the obvious one)
- Amplex and mints (for post-lunch halitosis)
- boss's favourite cigars/cigarettes/lipstick
- secret cache of office supplies (no matter how early you submit your order, you are always liable to find yourself without a printing cartridge or Prittstick)
- screwdrivers (small for spectacles, medium for plugs) though tweezers do most jobs as well
- 5 and 13 amp fuses
- boss's Beatrix Potter mug for moments of anxiety
- dry-cleaning fluid
- emergency telephone numbers: hotel, restaurant, massage parlour, sports club, and any local pub or wine bar in which your boss is apt to linger at the most inopportune moments
- list of boss's family birthdays, likes and dislikes and the presents you chose for them last year
- a selection of photographs for display on the boss's desk at appropriate times: for example, the visiting MD of an important client firm may be a horse racing fanatic – so a tasteful horsey photograph could be placed on the boss's desk just before the meeting. You may also wish to keep a stock of photographs of present and former girl/boyfriends or husbands/wives if your boss's personal affections are in a continual state of flux

- your own business cards to hand out to all those important contacts. It doesn't cost much to have them printed and works wonders for your image as a top professional.

Conquering Electronic Equipment

If you know very little about HTML or local area networks, well frankly, you ought to. But if you don't, help is at hand. Such is the desperate shortage of secretaries that colleges, agencies and even companies often provide free training.

The world of office electronics is still relatively elitist: you have to work hard at it to be an expert. If you can't be bothered, pick up what you can and vamp the rest. If you stick to what you know you will be just fine. Just don't let yourself be ruled by your computer and all its lovely little functions; your boss probably already is. Meantime, here are a few notes to help:

Fax Machines
Still vital for all the 'instant' things that e-mail cannot cope with, like tabulated lists or documents whose presentation is important, or that *Cosmo* quiz for your friend Norah in Stoke on Trent. Make yourself the expert on how to deal with a paper jam or the 'delayed sending program' and you can be forgiven much else.

PCs
The hub of any office. The plus side is that few users get familiar with more than one-fifth of what the program offers, so there is endless scope here.

The drawbacks of computers are:
- they 'crash' at the most inconvenient moment
- if you try to e-mail something important to a client, you can be sure your systems won't be compatible
- bosses demand multiple revisions of everything – "It's so easy with a computer, isn't it?"
- if you forget to make a backup of your work, congratulations: you've lost the lot.

Desktop Publishing

Amazingly high-quality word-processing program involving graphics and a choice of typefaces. Many firms now produce their own publicity material this way, instead of using outside printers. If you can type and your boss can't, you are ideally placed to become the firm's desktop publishing expert and therefore completely indispensable.

Networks

A fancy name for lots of PCs linked up to each other, so they can exchange information and share resources (leading to fist-fights over whose turn it is to use the printer). The Internet is the biggest network in the world.

E-mail

The electronic transfer of information. Devotees call everything else snail-mail. They have obviously never had an important message diverted via Shanghai, Slovenia and Kalamazoo, reappearing some weeks later on a PC in Warrington with all the punctuation missing.

Gadgets and Gismos

If your boss aims to cultivate an 'upwardly-mobile' image, ensure he (it's usually he – female bosses are too busy being better than anyone else to waste time on gimmicks) will be well-equipped with a good selection of pretentious gadgets:

- carphone (to use while hurtling down the motorway)
- mobile phone (more of a necessity than a luxury)
- laptop computer (to balance shakily on a knee somewhere above the North Atlantic, while composing ungrammatical correspondence which you will later be required to correct)
- electronic organiser/fax/e-mail/voice recorder, notepad, calendar with alarms, etc. (incorporated into a mobile phone for the ultimate mine-is-bigger-than-yours factor). Any manager who has the spare time required to program and run one of these clearly hasn't got enough work to do. Give him some.

COMMUNICATING

Secretaries perform three vital functions every day of their working lives, namely:

1. Communicating
2. Organising people, things and information
3. Preventing bosses from doing anything you'd rather they didn't.

Of the three, the first is the most important because without it the other two functions are impossible. Organisations would simply fall apart without their lines of communication, and the best secretaries know exactly how to manipulate the system for optimum results.

The Paper Mountain

For every communication you write, the post will ensure that you receive six more, not forgetting the faxes and e-mails. Do not be daunted. If you operate a strict system, you can keep the mountain down to manageable proportions. An excellent rule of thumb to aim for is that any piece of paper should be handled only once. So, divide your paperwork into three piles:

1. **For action**
   Important documents which must be acted upon. If possible, take action immediately. If not, mark with details of what needs to be done, and pass on to your boss.

2. **For information**
   Read and file or destroy. Or initial and circulate.

3. **For reading**
   Not important enough to be read straightaway, nor so worthless you should throw out. Save in your file of non-urgent work for times when you aren't busy but need to look as if you are.

There is one other category which can come in useful from time to time: a Procrastination File. Sometimes a letter or memo generates a problem which, if tackled immediately, will take days of unremitting toil for very little benefit. On the other hand, you strongly suspect that if you do nothing for a day or two, the problem may well sort itself out unaided and all your work will have been in vain. Just be careful: it may save time, but it could be a potential time-bomb.

The Mighty Memo

Memos are the confetti of the office world. Operate a guiding policy best summed up as, 'If in doubt, throw it out'. At one time Marks & Spencer decided to get rid of any document which was not absolutely essential to the efficient running of the business and in the first year they eliminated an amazing 260,000 pieces of paper and card (some 120 tons). Sadly, no matter how hard you try, you will never manage to get rid of memos – paper or electronic. So learn to play the system like an expert:

- keep them short, and, if possible, intelligible

- deal with one main theme per memo – otherwise the reader will tend to remember only the first point

- operate a bring-forward system such as a note in the office diary on the day/week/month when a response is expected. Don't be vague: give a specific date by which you or your boss want a reply, leaving plenty of time to sort things out if there are delays.

- keep memos of important instructions given by you to your boss (or vice versa) so there is no question of 'ignorance' when the balloon goes up. Managers constantly receive information which alters their ideas in the interim. You need to be able to prove that when he or she says "But I never told you to do that" – they did.

Letters of Complaint

As with presents, it is better to send these than to receive them. But from time to time all secretaries have to deal with letters which demand redress for some real or imagined injustice. There are two things to do:

1. If in doubt, simply send a reply stating 'Thank you for your letter, which has been passed to the appropriate authority'. It's the perfect alibi, especially if there isn't an authority, appropriate or otherwise.

2. If the complaint could have legal implications (e.g. 'My little boy got one of your tin soldiers stuck up his nose and I'm going to sue you') make sure your boss passes it on to the company lawyers and customer services experts before any reply goes out. Don't just stick it at the back of the bring-forward file and hope the whole thing goes away.

Presentation

Business today demands clear, precise language which expresses a given message in the shortest possible form. Even if your English is excellent, be sure to invest in your own:

- dictionary (a good one, not one of those dog-eared pocket ones with misleading definitions)
- thesaurus
- book on business communications – one with sample letters that you can crib from
- etiquette reference book, such as Black's *Titles and Forms of Address* – so you can introduce your boss to a Dame, a Crown Prince or the Pope

and use them. No-one ever need know that you owe all your skills to Roget.

Never underestimate the importance of presentation. The world is full of people whose hobby it is to scan every letter they receive for mistakes and howlers which they collect and share with their friends. They are not to know (or care) that the letter was produced at 7 p.m. on a Friday, when your boss was dictating over your shoulder as you typed.

A single atrocious error could send your own – and your boss's – reputation plummeting. One poor departmental secretary, harassed beyond belief, once typed and circulated a memo stating: 'Any member of staff requiring a floppy dick should report to me'. If by some unlucky chance your own boss spots some small blunder, bluff your way out of it with: "Just testing!" You can then bring the fair copy you've "had all the time" (amended, and hot off the printer) for signature.

Always check everything before you send it out, no matter how rushed you are. Better still, if it's something that has to be perfect, give it to a colleague to check. Others see mistakes which you will miss no matter how many times you look. Then check it again in case he or she has sabotaged you. (The danger is that this procedure could go on ad infinitum.)

Talking to Your Boss

Establishing good communications with your boss is vital. Many older secretaries prefer to maintain a distance between themselves and their managers, but the trend today is for a much more egalitarian approach. It's not just a case of giving and taking orders, but of two-way flow – preferably flowing all your way.

Successful secretaries have no difficulty in expressing themselves, or getting what they want. To do this you should catch the mood and tone of a situation. Be familiar and deferential, casual and formal by turns – whatever is appropriate to the occasion and the person. Take control by establishing regular, almost habitual communication with your boss by means of office 'summits' which take the form of:

a) two short sessions held at the start or end of each day (preferably both)

b) a longer weekly meeting for planning and consolidation (preferably not in the wine bar nearby because you may not remember much next day).

Mastering the Telephone

To prevent the telephone taking over your working hours, treat it like a precision rifle: deadly accurate and extremely useful in an emergency. Here are a few helpful hints:

1. Set aside some time each day to make telephone calls in 'batches'.

2. Before you make a call, write down a few notes on what you want to say: that way you don't get distracted into talking about other things.

3. If calling on behalf of your boss, find out in advance exactly what he or she wants from the call. An untrained boss will wait until you've done it and reported back, and then say: "Ah... Well, actually, I really wanted you to find out about such and such."

4. To keep calls brief, try calling in the late afternoon when people want to finish their work and go home. Or get yourself an egg-timer.

5. Never leave messages. It's a waste of time. Call back 10 times if you have to, but only speak to the person you want, not a substitute.

6. Refuse to have anything to do with video phones. It's bad enough having to sound convincing without having to look as if you mean what you say.

As for telephone etiquette, the convention is that if it's your boss's call, your opposite number will pass your boss through to her boss; if her boss calls yours, you wait until you have him on the line and then pass him through. Don't be outwitted by the opposition.

Because it is prestigious for callers to speak first to you, bosses are usually reluctant to answer the telephone themselves. This is where you have the edge: you are expert on the telephone, and can make it do anything you want, or appear to. Your boss should marvel as you decipher an incomprehensible Telecom manual with ease, and reprogram the switchboard to play *Greensleeves*.

But technical expertise is not the only jewel in the secretarial crown. Your real value on the telephone lies in manipulating people and so protecting your own and your boss's interests. A secretary's telephone skills should include the ability:

- to detect any facial expression merely by the sound of someone's voice
- to lie with consummate artistry
- to intimidate people without using a raised voice
- to stand ground and never give way
- to seduce. This technique has the power to reduce any irate caller (be it an old lady or the US President) to a state of confused but harmless benevolence, and persuade anybody to do, say or buy anything, even if they don't want to. This is done by smiling down the telephone (it really does change the way your voice sounds) and positively purring with reasonableness. It never fails.

Getting to Grips with the Grapevine

The office 'grapevine' may just be a glorified name for gossip, but it's effective and can be valuable to you. It can spread information like wildfire. A poll, carried out to see how employees got their information, revealed that in one company no fewer than 45 per cent of the employees felt that most news reached them this way.

There are, of course, drawbacks to using the grapevine if you want a reliable communications network. It's a great breeding-ground for distortion and delicious tittle-tattle. On the other hand, even wild rumours are actually believed by the people who hear them – so if you have always wanted to start your own rumour, this is not a bad way to do it.

The following strategies might be necessary from time to time:

a) **For the Boardroom Bigmouth**
Allow a 'draft' memo to fall, briefly, into the hands of the person concerned. The content must be highly controversial and, of course, entirely spurious. When it is 'leaked' before the next Board meeting, the bigmouth will look extremely foolish.

b) **For the Nosey Parker**
The shorthand in your notebook can be displayed expressly for the person whose nose is never out of other people's business. For the benefit of a busybody who can't read shorthand insert a few significant words in longhand into the text – words like 'redundancy' or 'fraud squad investigation' – with or without the name of the offender. Leaving something scurrilous on your computer screen works well, too. Snoopers can never resist a peek.

Handling VIPs

Secretaries deal with VIPs every day, sometimes without even realising it. Not all VIPs are cast in the Joan Collins or Donald Trump mould. Someone who wears brocade waistcoats and drives a Porsche is not necessarily more important to you than the person who hoovers the office. The most important people in your working life should be:

a) those who can help to make it easier and more pleasant

b) those who can help to keep your boss happy

c) those whose good opinion of you could influence your boss (and maybe result in promotion)

d) those who could really make your life a misery if they wanted to, who must of course be neutralised.

Treating everyone courteously is always a wise move; you never know if someone who is out of favour today might become flavour of the month tomorrow. But you can't be equally nice to everybody all the time; if you start doing too many favours you will simply gain a reputation as a prize mug. So be selectively unctuous. Here is a brief list of those to cultivate:

Your Boss
As long as you are a paragon of virtue in the eyes of your boss, not much else matters.

The One Who Mends (your PC/phone/etc.)
Maintenance men (and women) are the only safety net between the electronic office and disaster, and there aren't enough of them to go round. So next time the office terminal goes down and everything is in

chaos, ask yourself why he or she isn't in any hurry to rush to your rescue. Maybe if you had offered coffee in the past...

The Switchboard Operator/Receptionist

Make allies of these individuals; they can get their own back on you at every opportunity. A friendly receptionist and telephonist (in many organisations one and the same person) is a huge asset: messages can be taken, undesirable visitors blocked, favours done and important guests cossetted.

Anyone who has tried running a reception office whilst operating a multi-line switchboard and carrying out numerous secretarial tasks will tell you it's no holiday. Having some arrogant secretary say she's been waiting 10 minutes for a line out is a pain. If you are that secretary, you can expect to wait at least a further 30 minutes whilst the operator ensures that you do not get one. The occasional "thank you" works wonders in terms of goodwill.

Other Secretaries

You cannot be expected to be equally friendly with all your secretarial colleagues, but it is good policy to keep on the best possible terms – just as it's in their interests to try and remain friendly with you. This is because you all have stacks of useful information which you can share and exchange: for example, you may need to be sure that a certain restaurant is just the place for that impromptu business lunch.

Here are a few of the common species of secretary to be found in offices everywhere. Dedicated bluffers will need to be able to recognise and deal with them all:

● **The Dragon**. A fearsome beast. Of advancing years, usually to be found sensibly dressed and lying in wait for unsuspecting visitors who are mercilessly driven away from the inner sanctum.

- **Dumb Blonde**. Of limited intellect, but kept by enthusiasts for its exquisite plumage. Has a shrill, insistent cry and is liable to become confused very easily.

- **The Single Parent**. Fatigued but extremely industrious. Works frantically to sustain the barest levels of subsistence for its hungry brood. Often runs the company single-handed, without complaint.

- **The PA** (also known as the Management Assistant). Designer plumage. Believes itself to be a cut above its peers, and refuses to be called a secretary even though its qualifications and experience are exclusively secretarial.

- **The Predator**. Sports a degree (maybe two). Has the highest qualifications in the entire company and utter contempt for its boss. Biding its time, and waiting for an opportunity to be the boss.

- **Mr Role-Reversal**. Takes a fiendish delight in telling his male friends that he is a secretary (and earns far more than any of them). Stunningly efficient in the traditional skills of shorthand, typing and darning, and can master any computer system within half an hour.

Senior Managers/Other Companies
You never know when you might want another job, and the links you build up with other firms can only help your career.

Despatch/Bike Companies
The red corpuscles in the arteries of commerce. Alienate the booking staff and your boss's urgent deliveries will be lost, stolen, squashed or held up by traffic. Make friends, and you will always be first on the list.

The Tea Lady
If a tea lady likes you she will die for you. She will produce plates of mouthwatering canapés and pots of Earl Grey at five minutes' notice and in times of crisis is willing to don a uniform and do the full silver service bit. If she dislikes you, you can be sure that there will be cigarette ash on the biscuits and the coffee will arrive late and stone cold.

Cleaners
Cleaners know everything. If you can maintain good relations with your firm's janitorial staff you can be sure of hearing all the latest gossip before it even gets as far as the grapevine. It's amazing what can be deduced from the contents of people's wastepaper baskets. Your office will be spotless, too.

The Corporate Spouse
The only good corporate spouse is the one who keeps his or her nose out of your office. Most managers have spouses. These can be husbands or wives, close friends, mistresses or live-in-lovers – they all exert the same level of influence on your boss.

Corporate husbands are seldom a problem, but corporate wives are often possessed of a fiendish brand of low cunning, coupled with the bullying skills of a fishwife. Those who are intelligent, or think they are, are a danger to the smooth running of the office. The last thing you want is someone who once took a typing course telling your boss that you're doing it all wrong and insisting that the office be reorganised.

Things to remember when dealing with corporate spouses are:

– Always be polite but ever-so-slightly distant: get too friendly and you will find yourself making a daily visit to the cleaners on her or his behalf.
– Try not to look too glamorous when your boss's wife is around, or she may start imagining you have designs on her meal ticket. It helps to mention the man in your life – even if you haven't got one.
– Train your boss to understand that home and office are two separate places, and never the twain shall meet. If your boss's wife realises she is offending her husband by making continual disruptive visits to the office, she may stop doing it. If she knows she is annoying you, she will only do it even more.

The ones not worth bothering about:

The Shareholders: they may own the company, but they couldn't care less about you. Besides which, it's your boss who will get the blame if the company goes under.

Most Other Bosses: it's as well to be pleasant to your boss's fellow managers – you never know when your boss might be 'downsized'. But you don't have to be too chummy.

Junior Managers: they look down on you but in fact rely on you for their survival. They are largely to be ignored, with the possible exception of the whiz kid who is going straight to the top and wants to take you there too.

Fending and Defending

Your ability to say 'no' in the nicest possible way, and to neutralise the slickest sales patter with a cheerful barrage of facts and reasonableness makes you a formidable opponent for the troublemaker or the opportunist sales rep.

Techniques to employ vary according to personality and circumstances. Keep a 'library' of different approaches and use them on a mix and match basis. Some of the favourite manifestations are:

The Brick Wall: a well-known technique of the medical receptionist. The aim is to protect the boss (in this case the GP) from unwanted visitors (sick people). No matter what they say, if they don't have an appointment they will be treated to a stony glare over the top of the bifocals that implies: 'Well, you don't look ill to me', followed by any one of these dismissive statements:

- the only person authorised to buy anything from you is out of the country and won't be back for at least a month. You'll have to ring nearer the time to make an appointment.
- we never see anyone without an appointment, and all our managers are booked up for the next fortnight.
- leave your card, and someone will contact you – if we're interested in talking to you.
- leave some of your product literature, and I'll ensure that it is circulated to the people concerned.

'Pravda': not quite a lie, but not exactly the truth either. A good tool of diplomacy, since you cannot be proved to have lied to your visitor even though what you said was deliberately misleading.

Variations on this one are **The Barefaced Liar** (a technique, perfected by fiercely loyal secretaries, which demands forward planning and intelligence to ensure that you will not be caught out at some future date) and **Dumbo** which means saying nothing, although you may talk for hours. A good secretary should always know enough to be able to avoid giving out important facts accidentally. If in doubt, say nowt. You may appear brainless, but it's better than losing your job because you can't keep information to yourself. If you keep your wits about you even the most persistent reporter will give up in the end.

The Vile Seducer: a method for soothing savage beasts and manipulating awkward customers. This is an essential part of your armoury because secretaries are the magnet towards which all acrimony is directed, the boss having retreated to the golf course hours before. Smile a lot, maintain eye contact and pitch your voice low and soft. The essence of this one is apparent submissiveness: it hardly ever fails. Just remember never to raise your voice. Even if the other person is yelling and shouting at you, the minute you rise to the bait, you've lost the struggle.

The Sage: a variation of the Vile Seducer, but this time based on relentless reasonableness. The aim here is not to 'seduce' your opponent into a state of benevolence, but simply to present such a sensible aspect that he or she hasn't a leg to stand on.

The Oracle: if you are armed to the teeth with verifiable facts, you cannot be caught out. So long as you really do know everything, you will never be browbeaten by people who merely think they do.

The General: faultlessly polite but dedicated to the proper procedure. This quasi-military approach is not really appropriate for use by secretaries, but that need not stop you trying. It consists of reducing the essential flexibility of commercial life to a set of rules which nobody can possibly follow.

Playing Hostess

There will always be occasions when a secretary has to play the part of hostess. Just how big a part you play in this social side of business life will depend on:

a) the importance your boss places on entertaining
b) whether there are any incentives (overtime pay, time off or substantial 'goodwill')
c) whether or not you enjoy it.

It is as well to avoid taking on more than you had bargained for. Here are a few universal rules:

1. Be sure to extract as much notice as possible: if you know your boss well and have your finger on the corporate pulse, you should be able to anticipate the Imminent Function and confront your boss with the idea before he or she has had a chance to mention it. This way, you are in control and have time to devise a survival strategy for the occasion.

2. Avoid doing everything yourself. If your boss says "Can you do the catering for this one?", say "Yes, of course...but I think it would be advisable to get in an outside firm – I've been recommended a young company who are eager for work and very reasonable." Then make enquiries (or ring up a friend

who is in the cooking business and will be grateful for the opportunity). If it doesn't turn out as expected, you can always blame your 'source'.

3. Keep an ongoing list of caterers for future use, highlighting those who help out at short notice.

4. Get help from your opposite number. (What does Sir so-and-so like talking about? Would Lady X object to sitting next to Mr Y?) Swap tips and good/bad experiences of caterers, and you will be able to call in favours when you need to.

Business entertaining does not consist simply of two managers exchanging expense account favours in an exclusive restaurant. Here is a guide to some of the social functions you may encounter:

The Cocktail Party/Launch Party

This means hoards of people squashed into an art gallery, bookshop or whatever, trying to rub shoulders with the important guest(s). Food may be woefully inadequate (sculptured crudités, canapés, etc.), but wine will flow freely: glasses are topped up on demand and contracts can be made and lost in an alcoholic haze. Beware the professional drunk (often a gatecrasher) with a glass in each hand and an unerring talent for dropping his sausage-on-a-stick down another guest's cleavage. Your function is to ensure that he makes no attempt to rescue it.

The Buffet

The ideal opportunity to mingle, provided you are invited. Many a secretary has toiled long and hard to organise a buffet, only to spend the afternoon sulking at her desk, trying not to listen to the gales of laughter drifting down the corridor from the Board Room. Let it be known that the guests include three vegans and a person who requires kosher food, and that only you know which is which.

The Slap-up Do

Much beloved of the average male whose ideal lunch is likely to consist of a collection of jumbo rolls, gala pie, a big bowl of pork scratchings and a crate of Carlsberg Special – with a few bags of crisps for the ladies. Beware the urge to innovate and 'improve': your boss and his guests like it this way, besides which this is the very easiest sort of 'do' to organise.

The Corporate Hand-out

A phenomenon which becomes more and more common as interest rates rise. Executives who are mortgaged to the hilt and have four children at public school view company lunches as an ideal opportunity for a free feed. Some are so desperate that they will even volunteer their services at irrelevant meetings and conferences, just so they can get their teeth into the feast afterwards. They can be seen sneaking away from the venue, their briefcases crammed with chicken drumsticks. It's not a very public spirited way to behave, but if everyone's doing it, you might as well bag that big Stilton.

The Farewell Feed

Uncomfortable occasions when the firm says goodbye to Jack or Emily after 35 years of unselfish toil, and management tries to avoid contentious issues – such as the fact that Jack has been made redundant and doesn't want to leave.

For his part, Jack will do his best to introduce a note of bitter sarcasm into his speech – perhaps spiced with a few revelations about the Chief Accountant – as he accepts his extremely small leaving present and checks to see who hasn't signed his card. Your role is to keep the chief antagonists apart and see that the flow of alcohol cauterises the wounds. If the person who has been made redundant is your boss, make sure you get your share because you're probably next.

Public Sector Hospitality
The big problems here are lack of money, expertise and a suitable space (a school canteen, a staff commonroom or a Portakabin). Taking an enthusiastic or stylish approach is generally frowned upon, and bringing in outside caterers is unthinkable (unless one can be found who will do the job for 60p a head) so Mrs Jones the Assistant Cook is usually expected to do something creative with a pound of Cheddar, two pickled onions and a large white, sliced. Your job is to divert the guests' attention from such paucity of vision and to go round asking all your colleagues to say they aren't hungry when the cake arrives, because there's only enough for the guests.

The Sit Down Do
Sometimes company funds will run to a full three- or four-course meal. Your job will consist of:

– sending out invitations and monitoring responses
– dealing with internal or external caterers

- ensuring the meal is balanced and within budget (if you don't know what to choose and most of the guests are men, go for fish – it never fails)
- drawing up a seating plan (and making little name cards so that if it isn't a howling success you can say they swopped places)
- liaising with the secretaries of your important guests to make sure that allowances are made for all their little peccadillos.

The Christmas Party

A great many office Christmas parties are organised by secretaries. This is because secretaries are good at organising things and are often foolish enough to volunteer for the job in a rash moment of pre-festive goodwill.

If you are tempted, remember that 90 per cent of misunderstandings seem to originate somewhere in the depths of one of these infamous occasions. If you attend, never drink too much. A glass of Perrier with a slice of lemon in it looks remarkably like a gin and tonic, and whilst you're in full control of your faculties you can keep an eye on your boss, as well as fend off inebriated reps and spotty accounts clerks.

You need not worry if bosses make fools of themselves in front of the entire office, announcing to the Chairman's wife that they intend to stand on the table and do the strip sequence from *The Full Monty*. Just make sure it isn't your boss who is tempted to be the star turn. Those who suddenly realise the following day that their secretaries have saved their reputations will have a massive debt of gratitude to pay. Don't be in too much of a hurry to let them pay it off.

TRAINING YOUR BOSS

A well-trained boss is a credit to a secretary, the organisation, and the envy of all the other secretaries in the organisation. An untrained – or worse, a badly trained – boss is nothing short of a liability.

There is an apocryphal story about a boss who was so determined to be in control of his office that he opened, read and replied to every item of incoming mail, no matter how trivial. So obsessive and distrustful was he that when he went away on holiday he made his secretary travel to and from the office each day, to bring him the mail. He is an extreme type, but he is not alone. Here are some other types which you may recognise:

The Offloader. Gets rid of all the boring or difficult jobs which he doesn't want to do himself by giving them to his secretary and calling it delegation. She gets all the blame if things go wrong, but if there's any credit going, it's all his. Disappears like magic whenever a crisis looms.

The One Man Band. Determined to do absolutely everything himself, even if it kills him. His motto is: if you want a job doing properly, you have to do it yourself. Won't even give his secretary the authority to order a box of paper clips without looking over her shoulder as she fills in the requisition. Tends to shield his work from sight when you walk in.

The Lord High Executioner. Glares at the world from behind his mahogany desk, and makes it his policy to shout at everyone at least once a day. Is invariably right. If any project proves successful, it was entirely his idea.

The Self-Made Man. Joined the firm as tea boy and worked his way up from the shop floor. Tells everyone he got all his education at the University of Life. Likes to use long words but doesn't know what they mean. Thinks he can spell.

The Playboy. A confirmed male chauvinist pig. The only figure work he is interested in is yours. His conversation is peppered with innuendoes, but he would probably run a mile if you took him up on any of his offers. Generally married and going bald.

The Wimp. A Peter Pan figure who will never grow into his job because it will always be far too big for him. Usually found sheltering behind Wendy – a fiercely competent secretary who would die rather than reveal his shortcomings.

The Organiser. Organises everything and everybody. Spends several hours each day with a collection of Filofaxes (one is not enough), writing lists of things he or she won't have time to do.

The Amazon. A she-devil in designer trousers who has got to the top by sheer strength of purpose. Smokes a hundred cigarettes a day (three at once). A veritable slave driver, with no sympathy for human frailty. Be prepared to take lessons.

Mother Earth. Has several small children and a handbag full of wet wipes and half-chewed fruitgums. Appears vague and disorganised on the surface, but is in fact frighteningly intelligent, and more than able to hold her own in the UN Security Council. Underestimate her at your peril: no crisis is too daunting for a woman who has potty-trained triplets.

Devising a Training Programme

Breaking in a new boss is a bit like learning how to use a new keyboard: once you've mastered the basic controls, you wonder why there was ever a problem.

Here are the signs of a boss who is in need of urgent training.

Untrained Boss

Incapable of organising anything. Suddenly realises at 5.15 pm that there are 10 urgent tasks for you to complete, today. So you have to stay late.

Considers the telephone your province. Has made no attempt to master new call-connect system. This boss's idea of a message is: 'Somebody called. Has a very deep voice'.

Demands to know why you spend so much time in the lavatory.

Sees having a secretary as a golden opportunity to offload all those rotten, routine jobs that are felt to be beneath his or her dignity.

Trained Boss

Organises tasks so that you have an even workload and can plan for the week ahead.

Knows how to answer the telephone and is happy to do so when you are not in the office. Faultlessly polite and efficient message-taker – of your social events.

Accepts your feeblest excuse without question.

Accepts 'delegated' work from you without complaint and makes brave attempt to type the odd label while pretending to keep in touch with modern technology.

Keeps everything close to the chest yet expects you to know exactly what is going on.

Makes time to fill you in on everything at a daily conference. Look interested and try not to yawn.

Says any fool can type and believes e-mail will soon render secretaries obsolete, saving millions.

Respects your skills: "I don't know how I'd manage without you to organise my life."

Takes credit for everything, including successes which are entirely due to you.

Makes sure you get the credit you deserve.

When things don't go quite to plan, it's all your fault.

Nobly accepts blame when things go wrong.

Believes people become secretaries because they're too thick to do anything else.

Promotes your career and wants to help you get into management.

Does not trust you.

Allows you complete control of the office finances and his wallet, and lets you know where he keeps his pile ointment.

These are just a few of the common symptoms associated with untrained bosses. Bluffers will not be surprised to learn that some of the worst examples can be women. Those who used to be secretaries can seize the opportunity to take out years of resentment and subjugation on their own horrified secretaries. Worse, a woman boss knows all the dodges.

Women managers also tend to be extremely able, resilient and painfully demanding: perhaps this is why they are traditionally less popular with female secretaries than male managers are. If you find yourself working for one of these Imelda Marcos-style paragons, the best you can do is grit your teeth, play by the rules and learn.

With less hopeless cases, there is a great deal you can do to make your life easier. Here are the basic items to include in your boss's training programme:

Dictation

The shorthand speeds which firms ask for in job advertisements are largely arbitrary figures, plucked at random from other job advertisements. Fortunately many managers have a very hazy idea of what secretaries do all day, let alone the sort of speeds at which they will be expected to take dictation. The average boss has received no training whatsoever in dictation skills, and a figure such as 100 words per minute conveys about as much meaning as a railway timetable in Chinese.

Every manager has his or her own style of dictation. There are those who speak so slowly that you could take everything down in longhand; those who gabble at 160 wpm; those who are inaudible; those who wander about, or dictate with their heads stuck out of the window, and those who are so lacking in confidence that they write everything down and pretend to dictate spontaneously as they read from a sheet held surreptitiously beneath the desk.

None of this will do. It is bad enough trying to cope with pens that suddenly run out, interruptions, or an impenetrable accent without also having to interject a "Do you mean ...?", or similar sort of red herring, so you can catch up.

A few training sessions will soon set your boss on the right track. Concentrate on teaching him or her:

– to find a comfortable and practicable speed
– to agree on who will provide punctuation and para-graphing: either that you will put it all in yourself, or that your boss gives you every comma. A mix-ture of the two will only lead to confusion.
– to give you all the documentation relating to a letter or memo – so you can check names, addresses, etc., before typing.

Never take dictation when your boss is in a temper. Anything dictated in this frame of mind is likely to impair his or her judgement. If you cannot forestall the answering of an abusive letter, or if there is any-thing you are not happy with, you should hold it back until the next day. You can say the post went early and then place the offending article under your boss's nose. Most people can't resist taking a second look, and the chances are that anything litigious or illiterate will be safely consigned to the shredding machine.

Confused copy often results from audio dictation. There seems to be a gremlin which scrambles the words between the tape and the keyboard. This isn't always the secretary's fault. Audio dictation brings out the very worst in most managers. Dictating a letter whilst running to catch a train, or eating a smoked salmon sandwich, does little to improve verbal clarity. A complete disregard for rhythm doesn't help either. One Glaswegian eye surgeon dictated at top speed, pausing only very occasionally and always in the middle of sentences. The result was that most of the letters produced by his many temporary secre-taries looked like avant-garde prose poems.

If your boss must use audio, impose these rules:

- do not dictate whilst running, eating, blowing your nose or operating noisy machinery
- do not hold the microphone at arm's length (or pressed against the mouth), or wander away from it whilst dictating
- do not start dictating before the tape has started running properly or carry on after it has run out.

There is one other foible that you will never prevent, so it's best to be wise to it. Always run the tape right through first so you hear the vital instruction, tacked on the end, to "Cancel that last letter" – and are thus saved from doing it in the first place.

Diaries

Secretaries are supposed to know where their bosses are at all times. When this is not the case, it is usually because their managers forget to tell them where they are. If you leave the office, delegating telephone duties to your boss, be careful to check that no appointments have been made without your knowledge. Left to their own devices, managers are bound to make calls, fix dates and pencil them into their own pocket diaries. The solutions are to:

a) train your boss to tell you everything that has occurred in your absence

b) confiscate your boss's pocket diary at the end of every working day and scan it for evidence (he or she will always try to sneak something in, even when you're there)

c) scold (it probably won't help much, but it might make you feel better).

Deception

Deception is an important part of office politics and is really the art of bluff taken to its logical extreme. It is one of the secretary's most necessary skills.

Never let your boss place you in an awkward situation where you have to come up with an instant, 'off-the-cuff' lie. Discuss tactics before it happens. See that your stories tally and draw up contingency plans. If your boss is going to spend the afternoon engaged in some frivolous pursuit, you need to know details of when and where and how to get in touch, just in case something really urgent crops up. After all, 'secretary' means 'one who keeps secrets'.

Failure to collude could turn a loyal attempt to cover up into a fiasco. Imagine the repercussions when you tell the Board that your boss is at the dentist, only to be contradicted when the Chairman spots your boss on Match of the Day, as part of the happy, tanned crowd at Wimbledon. So insist that your boss be open and honest – at least with you.

Delegation

Secretaries are the real managers in any office. The managers themselves are not there to deal with day-to-day organisational or administrative matters, and indeed often have no ability in these areas.

What you have to do is teach your boss to let go: to delegate some of the more interesting and challenging problems to you, stand well back and let you show just what you can do. Meantime, never let an opportunity pass by for delegating anything mundane or difficult, to your boss.

The Golden Rule to instil when training your manager is this: when in doubt, leave it to the expert – you.

Some Do's and Don'ts

- Don't admit to all your qualifications – at least not all at once – or your boss will feel threatened, and won't trust you any more.

- Do produce work of a brilliant standard – but not too often, or your boss will come to expect it. What is more, the better you are at being a secretary, the more likelihood there is that you will remain one.

- Do drop hints about your delicate state of health ("I have this little problem which is difficult to discuss"). Your boss will be more understanding when it recurs at strategic moments.

- Do let your boss make use of your skills, but noise it abroad in an innocent way ("I did my best with that and found that he/she actually used it").

- Do make sure your boss notices when you've done something particularly well. It's no use working your socks off if the people who matter don't know you exist.

- Do devise some handy code words for confidential messages (verbal or written) between you and your boss. No-one will ever suspect that 'Contact Headingly office by 5 p.m.' really means England have lost the Test match by five wickets.

- Don't make the mistake of revealing your own special systems. During your absences the office will subside into chaos and your boss will believe you have supernatural powers.

CHANGING YOUR JOB

At the best of times choosing a new job is something of a minefield. You may hate the job you've got, but what if the next one is worse? What is more, it takes time and effort to train a boss properly. Just when you've established the proper office relationship (he gets to sit behind the mahogany desk but you run the show), you move to a new job and find you have inherited a completely untrained boss.

On the other hand, if you are going to be a top secretary you have to move on. Company loyalty is all very well, but remaining with United Surgical Stockings Ltd for the duration of your career is not a good idea. Many a secretary has stayed loyal to one boss for years on end, assuming that loyalty would lead to promotion. All too many have found themselves redundant at 45 – the victims of their bosses' retirement or the menopause (theirs or yours).

Whatever the reasons you give a prospective employer for leaving (you want to develop your full potential/change fields/broaden your outlook/meet a new challenge), there are many genuine reasons why you might consider looking for a new job:

1. Your boss is moving, and his successor will almost certainly bring his secretary with him – so you could find yourself demoted.

2. Your boss has made a serious error of judgement or has a sudden fall from grace. Better for you to move on before he gets dismissed (especially if the error of judgement had something to do with you).

3. Your boss is not responding to standard training techniques. Some bosses are simply untrainable, and are not worth the effort.

4. Your boss has started to snap at you. The whole idea is to remain aloof yet fascinating, so that your boss's interest in your wellbeing does not flag. When familiarity allows the mystique to be destroyed he or she may begin to notice that you have certain flaws. The minute that happens, it's time to move on.

5. You have started to despise your boss's inadequacies. Find yourself a boss you can respect, or you just won't be motivated to do your job properly – and you'll never get promoted.

6. You want more money.

7. You want to get to the top.

Agencies

Employment agencies are the bane of a professional secretary's life. They provide a useful service, yet they are often unbearably persistent and pushy.

In their favour:

a) they carry large numbers of job vacancies, many of which don't find their way into newspapers

b) specialist agencies can help you find a job in exactly the right industry or environment

c) they can usually fix interviews within hours or days

d) they sometimes offer training (e.g. on WP systems) if they think you will agree to temp for them

e) they have the knowhow and the contacts to market your skills and experience, and can say glamorous things about you that you cannot say yourself.

To their detriment:

a) they are staffed by hard-faced individuals whose sole aim in life is to persuade you to take a job, even if it's patently unsuitable. If they place you they receive a fat commission: the more people they place, the higher their salary. So beware the hard sell.

b) they are obsessed by speeds and tests. Even if you have been PA to the Chief Executive Officer of IBM for 10 years, the minute you walk into an agency you will be asked to take a typing test. If you refuse, they may not take you on. Some agencies go right over the top and submit all their applicants to spelling, proof-reading and word comprehension tests. Bluffers should submit with good grace, do a minute's worth, and then quit. When challenged to do more, simply claim that this is all that is required elsewhere.

c) they place spurious job advertisements in newspapers. For example: 'Job of a lifetime with international film company for enthusiastic WP sec: no shorthand'. Thus the agency receives dozens of calls from secretaries desperate to work for Spielberg or meet George Clooney. But all applicants are told: "Sorry – that job's gone. But we do have lots of other positions which could interest you...". In fact, the job never existed: it was simply a lure to attract potential custom.

So never take anything that an agency tells you at face value. Always ask yourself, "What's in it for them?"

The Job Ads Jungle

Employers adopt some pretty desperate measures to attract the sort of secretarial staff they want. Most people who write job ads don't actually resort to lying, but they can be very economical with the truth. Here are a few examples to help guide you through the jungle:

The Money

salary not stated/salary negotiable at interview	they want to see how little you are prepared to work for
competitive salary/ attractive salary	low salary (so low you wouldn't have applied if they quoted it)
big bucks/megabucks	an appeal to basic human greed (salary not that impressive or they would have quoted it)
fantastic salary	so low you won't believe it
salary according to age and experience	the younger you are, the better: then they can pay you peanuts
good salary for the right applicant	your idea of 'good' will not be the same as theirs

The Job

great staff benefits	minimum value luncheon vouchers
free lunch	count on the carbohydrates in the canteen as the area is devoid of all amenities

friendly environment	sloppy and inefficient methods
dynamic company	a) the boss is even younger than you are b) there's a strong chance they could go bust c) they're American
good prospects	there might be a way out but in the meantime you have to bear it
varied duties	a) we don't know what they are yet b) accept this job and you could be letting yourself in for anything c) you're going to have to do everything your boss doesn't want to do d) you will photocopy computer sheets and take the mail daily to the post office
demanding job	a) we're going to work you until you drop b) you have to cover for a boss who can't cope
not a 9–5 job	long hours, no overtime pay
would suit 1st or 2nd jobber	a) we want somebody 16-18 b) if you're any older than that, don't expect any more money
high-flying PA	a) don't apply if you're over 35 b) we want shorthand c) be prepared to walk up five flights of stairs

The Candidate

Applicants should be:

adaptable/flexible	a) the boss is always changing his/her mind for no reason
	b) nobody stays for long
content to work alone/ with minimal supervision/ on own initiative/	the boss is always out and you have to fend off people who want their bills paid
lively/bright/enthusiastic/ full of fun/outgoing	young, pretty, and a pushover at the firm's annual outing
mature	a) over 18, under 35
	b) no threat
	c) getting a pension so can't be paid much
willing/hardworking	a drudge
patient/tactful/sensitive	the boss is a monster and has marital problems
calm/level-headed, full of common sense	the boss is neurotic and can't cope with emergencies
computer literate	we've just upgraded and no-one understands the programme
competent/with sound secretarial skills	no more, no less– we're not made of money
apply with CV and recent photograph	if you're not pretty, don't bother

Temping

Temping used to be seen as exciting, lucrative and slightly sexy. Agencies would like you to believe it still is. But once they have lured you in you will rapidly discover that you are not regarded as some sort of freelance saint. A temp is still a dogsbody, and very firmly bottom of the heap.

Temping may not be the perfect long-term career, but it's a great way to 'fill in' between jobs. To the indecisive it's a godsend because all those varied assignments give you ample opportunity to test the water before you take the plunge. Some of the points to bear in mind before signing up are:

a) Temps never have much status amongst their permanent colleagues yet are expected to be just as good as the permanent holder of the job. If the permanent secretary is a bluffer like you, chances are you won't be left much information to help you.

b) some temping jobs arise because the boss is such an ogre that no permanent staff will stay. Don't let the agency bully you into staying longer because "you're so good and we're so short of temps".

d) no matter how hard agencies try to make you feel as if you are a 'career secretary', you aren't. Paid holidays are a help, but if you really want to progress, you have to get out of temping and get into a permanent job with prospects. The problem is that you might have to take a pay cut – and good money can be addictive.

c) constantly being 'new' gives you little chance to settle in and develop good working relationships. On the other hand, it's one way to widen the potential for personal relationships.

Temps are infinitely expendable; but good ones can pick and choose. Just beware of:

1. the boss who offers you the same job on a permanent basis. In capital cities, temps earn far more per hour than permanent staff. If you transfer to a permanent contract you will probably suffer a massive drop in salary.

2. the boss who agrees to take you on permanently and then says, "Let's not tell the agency, eh?" This is defrauding the agency of its commission. They are bound to find out and if you ever want to temp again, you can forget it.

Your Working Environment

Readers of glossy business magazines might be forgiven for thinking that all secretaries today enjoy equal opulence in their working conditions: everything from cyberspace computers to ionisers, laser printers to luncheon vouchers. It isn't so. Ask any downtrodden Girl Friday. The age of the manilla folder and the manual typewriter is not yet dead.

Bluffer's should recognise at least three basic kinds of working environments:

The Small Business

This could be your big chance to run a business, single-handed. The only drawback is that you are unlikely to be paid accordingly. Many small-time business people can only afford to take on one administrative worker... you. Or at least, they say they can only afford you, and even then it's going to be a struggle, so would you mind taking a bit of a pay cut until they get the cash-flow problems sorted out?

Most individualists don't know much about typing, filing or VAT: that's *your* job. You will find yourself endowed with an awesome degree of responsibility whenever the boss is not in the office. Contracts could be won or lost on the way you handle a difficult client. There is no-one else to turn to for advice, so you learn quickly: secretaries who work in small businesses are renowned for their efficiency and resourcefulness, and it's hardly surprising.

So if you want experience and responsibility, this could be for you. The pay is not much good, but you might end up as a company director.

The Multinational

If it's money, deep pile carpets and designer living you're looking for, this is the place to be. Generally speaking, the bigger the organisation, the more secretarial jobs there are and the better the salary structure and promotion prospects.

However, in the world of business and high finance, only the best survive – and that applies to secretaries too. If you are really good, you can just about name your price and will probably be 'head-hunted' from time to time by your boss's business contacts. Achieve something noteworthy, and you will be justified in asking for – and getting – a bonus or a pay rise. On the other hand, regular appraisals will ensure that anyone who does not pull his or her weight will at best not stand a chance of promotion. Make a really bad mistake and (unless your loyal boss is willing to shoulder the responsibility) you could be out on your ear.

The Public Sector

Not so many years ago, the secretary who joined public service at 16, 18 or 21 was more or less assured of a long career, complete with pension and a gradually increasing holiday entitlement as the years of service were accumulated. Once in, doors were opened to better-paid and more prestigious secretarial posts, and those who were very determined and talented could cross the bridge from secretarial work into administrative grades.

Some of this is still true. But not much. There is no such thing as a job for life any more, and if it's big bucks and all the latest gismos you are after, public service is not for you.

Unfortunately pay is notoriously uncompetitive and working conditions can be a bit grim. Arcane rules and regulations can be irksome too if you are the sort of person who believes in flexibility and spontaneity. However, if you enjoy knowing exactly where you stand (and indeed where you are likely to be standing in ten years' time), the public sector could be just what you've been looking for.

Happily for less than competent bluffers, staff are rarely sacked for anything short of Treason or Gross Moral Turpitude.

Starting Your New Job

If you are going to make it as a top secretary you will need to establish the following:
a) a network of people (especially other secretaries) from whom you can call in favours
b) a position of power and influence

58

c) a secure place in the office grapevine
d) a 'public image' which combines integrity, charm, helpfulness and just the merest touch of ruthless determination.

These guidelines for your first few months are by no means foolproof, but they might help:

1. Be pleasant to everybody, no matter how rude they are to you. You can even the score later.

2. Don't get involved in any factions, or become too closely allied with anyone in particular. Save your confidences until you know people better.

3. On no account criticise anyone openly, even if they seem unbearably stupid or spiteful. That vulgar and unpleasant despatch man might just be the Chairman's old retainer, doing his best to supplement a pension.

4. Concentrate on doing your work competently – but make it clear that you feel as if you know nothing and would welcome help and advice.

5. Build up your own 'database' of useful information and addresses, and keep your eyes and ears open for intelligence about the way your new organisation really works, as opposed to the way it's supposed to work.

The big problem about settling in is that your predecessor may have done his or her level best to ensure that things are as confusing as possible for your arrival. Secretaries have been known to destroy files of vital information which they have built up over several years, simply to 'wrong-foot' the next person to do the job. The result is that their reputation becomes almost sacred to the manager: "X used to do this, so why can't you?" The best you can do is to get help from your colleagues and build up your own reputation – slowly.

A Strategy for Success

Never go into a job expecting it to be easy – but don't expect to do badly, either. Most people want to do well and progress, and since you are reading this book you are probably one of them. The main thing to remember is that working at full stretch, 100 per cent of the time, is not the ideal way to get promotion. You need a strategy, which could be summarised as follows:

1. Work hard for six months and don't get into any trouble (no personal phone calls at work; no arriving late and leaving early).

2. Back pedal: your reputation is established and you've got the hang of the job so you can let yourself coast for a while.

3. You want promotion. Work like crazy for six months and if you haven't been promoted by then, look for a new job outside the firm.

When considering success you might like to reflect on the following tale:

Mr A's secretary was surprised by the arrival of Mr B, a business colleague of her boss, a full day in advance of the date she had arranged for their meeting.

She suggested a mistake must have been made, but Mr B insisted that this was the day he had in his diary. "Well," she said, "I'm afraid a meeting couldn't have been fixed for today because it's Tuesday, and Mr A always spends Tuesdays in the City." "The whole day?" queried Mr B. "Yes," replied the secretary. "But," said Mr B in some alarm, "who runs the business in his absence?" and the secretary replied: "The same person who runs it when he's here."

If you enjoy being a secretary, are good at it and are well paid for what you do, then keep on bluffing and you'll get to the top. But if you dislike the job, try to get out before the magic age of 35. Failing that, fib about your age. Never forget the Personnel Manager's response when an agency offered him a secretary who was over 40: "Provided that's her bust measurement, no problem. Otherwise, forget it."

A Career for Life

This is the age of self-actualisation and Big Ambitions: everyone wants to be Number One. There is nothing to stop you being Number One too, but it's not easy in a job which by definition elects you as Number Two. Nevertheless, long gone are the days when a typical secretarial career looked something like this:

Age 15:   Leave school. Take secretarial course.

Age 16:   Leave college with certificates in shorthand, typing and book-keeping. Obtain job as office junior at Maggot, Slug and Earwig (solicitors and commissioners for oaths). Sweep a lot of floors; make tea; lick stamps.

Age 17: Promotion to junior secretary. When not getting electric shocks from antique switchboard, type letters all day facing a wall.

Age 18: Promotion to Mr Maggot's personal secretary. Buy navy crimplene suit and pluck eyebrows.

Age 19: Get married; become pregnant; leave work.

15 years later: Take refresher course. Get part-time job as shorthand-typist.

Nowadays the career path is likely to look rather more like this:

Age 18: Emerge from college with Private Secretary's Certificate and extensive ambitions. Split up with steady boyfriend because he doesn't like the idea of you earning more than he does. Obtain well-paid secretarial post immediately. Work extremely hard for six months.

Age 19: Bully boss into sending you on a self-assertion course. Assert yourself. Go on courses in self-defence and stress management.

Age 20: Send yourself on a course in 'Management for Secretaries'.

Age 21: Become pregnant. Refuse to get married. Employ former boyfriend as nanny. Return to work immediately.

Age 22: Promotion to management. Meteoric success.

Age 25: Sack former boss.

THE AUTHOR

Sue Dyson knows a lot about bluffing. In 1987 she accidentally became Secretary of the Year and has been bluffing ever since.

An experienced French translator, she spent several years translating letters to and from irate Breton pig farmers about their imploding grain silos. Finding that this was not sufficiently lucrative, she decided to train as a Secretary. The results were two gold medals, a crystal goblet and the highest marks ever awarded in the Private and Executive Secretary's Diploma examinations. She was suitably embarrassed and bought a blouse with a bow on the front to try to look the part.

She has since been a temp, a medical secretary, a secretary/receptionist in a technical college, a lecturer in shorthand, typing and management for secretaries, and now almost makes a living writing books. When she isn't writing, she sings (semi-professionally), collects Isle of Man seaside souvenirs, and dreams in shorthand.

THE BLUFFER'S GUIDES®

The million-copy best-selling series that contains facts, jargon and inside information – all you need to know to hold your own among experts.

Available titles:

Accountancy
Archaeology
Astrology &
  Fortune Telling
Chess
The Classics
Computers
Consultancy
Cricket
Doctoring
Economics
The EU
The Flight Deck
Golf
The Internet
Jazz
Law
Management
Marketing
Men
Music

Opera
Personal Finance
Philosophy
Public Speaking
The Quantum
  Universe
The Rock Business
Rugby
Science
Secretaries
Seduction
Sex
Skiing
Small Business
Stocks & Shares
Tax
Teaching
University
Whisky
Wine
Women

These books are available from your local bookshop (in the UK), or from the publishers:

Oval Books, 335 Kennington Road, London SE11 4QE.
Telephone: (0) 20 7582 7123; Fax: (0) 20 7582 1022
E-mail: info@ovalbooks.com